HAL•LEONARD
pro vocal 🔊
BETTER THAN KARAOKE!

SONGBOOK & 2 SOUND-ALIKE CDs
WITH UNIQUE *PITCH-CHANGER*™

WOMEN / MEN EDITION
VOLUME 9

More Songs from **glee**

Music From The FOX Tele...

Series Artwork, Fox Trademarks and Logos
TM and © 2010 Twentieth Century Fox Film Corporation
All Rights Reserved.

ISBN 978-1-4234-9801-8

HAL•LEONARD®
CORPORATION
7777 W. BLUEMOUND RD. P.O. BOX 13819 MILWAUKEE, WI 53213

For all works contained herein:
Unauthorized copying, arranging, adapting, recording, Internet posting, public performance,
or other distribution of the printed or recorded music in this publication is an infringement of copyright.
Infringers are liable under the law.

Visit Hal Leonard Online at
www.halleonard.com

CONTENTS
CD 1

CONTENTS
CD 2

Bad Romance

Words and Music by Stefani Germanotta and Nadir Khayat

Copyright © 2009 Sony/ATV Music Publishing LLC and House Of Gaga Publishing Inc.
All Rights Administered by Sony/ATV Music Publishing LLC, 8 Music Square West, Nashville, TN 37203
International Copyright Secured   All Rights Reserved

Chorus

F | G | Am

I want your love, and _ I want your re - venge, _ you and me ___ could write a bad ro - mance. _

C | F | G

___ I want your love, and all your lov-er's re - venge, _ you and me _

E/G# | Am *Male/Female:* | F

___ could write a bad ro - mance. _ Whoa, ___
3

G | Am | C

_____ caught in a bad ro - mance. _ Whoa, ___

F | G | E/G#

_____ 3 _____ caught in a bad ro - mance. _

Interlude

Am | Am/C Am/E Fmaj7 | Am Am/C Am/E Fmaj7

___ Rah, rah, ah, ah, ah, ___ ro - ma, ro - ma, ma, ___

Am Am/C Am/E Fmaj7 | G *Female:* | Am Am/C Am/E Fmaj7 *Male/Female:*

Ga - ga, ooh, la, la, ___ want your bad ro - mance. Rah, rah, ah, ah, ah, ___

Don't Rain on My Parade

from FUNNY GIRL
Words by Bob Merrill
Music by Jule Styne

Copyright © 1963 by Chappell & Co.
Copyright Renewed
International Copyright Secured   All Rights Reserved

Bridge 1

___ got-ta fly once, I ___ got-ta try once. On - ly can die once, right, sir? Ooh, ___ life ___ is ___ juic - y, ___ juic - y, and you see I ___ got-ta have my bite, sir. ___

Verse

Get read-y for me, love, 'cause I'm a com - er. I sim - ply got-ta march, my heart's ___ a drum - mer. Don't bring a - round a cloud to rain ___ on my _____ pa - rade. ___

Bridge 2

I'm gon - na live and ___ live now,

get what __ I want, I ____ know how.

One roll ____ for the whole _ she - bang,

one throw, _ that bell will ____ go clang.

Eye on ____ the tar - get ____ and wham,

one shot, ____ one gun - shot ____ and BAM.

Hey, Mis - ter Arn - stein, here I

am. ____

I'll march my

Dream On
Words and Music by Steven Tyler

Copyright © 1973 Music Of Stage Three
Copyright Renewed
All Rights Administered by Stage Three Music (U.S.) Inc.
All Rights Reserved   Used by Permission

Pre-Chorus 1

I know no-bod-y knows where it comes and where it goes.

I know ev-'ry-bod-y's sin; you got to lose to know how to

win. _____

Verse

Half my life's in books' writ-ten pag - es, lived and learned from

fools and from sag - es. You know it's true, _____

____ all the things _____ come back to you. _____

Pre-Chorus 2

____ Sing with me, sing for the year, ____ sing for the laugh-ter, sing ____ for the tear. ____

Sing it with me if it's just for to-day. ____ May-be to-mor - row the good Lord will take you a-way.

Yeah, _____ dream on, ___ dream on, ___

dream on, ___ dream on. ___ Dream on, ___ dream on, ___

dream on, ___ whoa. _____

Pre-Chorus 2

Sing it with me, sing for the year, _ sing for the laugh-ter, sing _ for the tear. _

Sing it with me if it's just for to-day. _ May-be to-mor - row the good Lord will take you a-way.

Pre-Chorus 2

___ Sing it with me, sing for the year, _ sing for the laugh-ter, sing _ for the tear. _

Sing it with me if it's just for to-day. _ May-be to-mor - row the good Lord will take you a-way, _

Outro

___ He'll take you a - way. _____

Faithfully

Words and Music by Jonathan Cain

Intro
Moderately slow

High-way run ___ in-to the mid-night sun; ___

Rest-less

wheels go round ___ and round, ___ you're on my mind. ___

hearts sleep a-lone to-night, ___ send-ing all ___ my love ___ a-long the

Copyright © 1983 Love Batch Music (ASCAP) and Weed-High Nightmare Music (ASCAP)
All Rights for Weed-High Nightmare Music Administered by Wixen Music Publishing Inc.
International Copyright Secured   All Rights Reserved

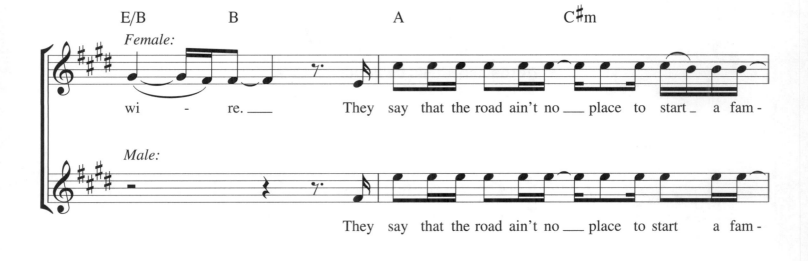

Female: wi - re. ___ They say that the road ain't no ___ place to start a fam-

Male: They say that the road ain't no ___ place to start a fam-

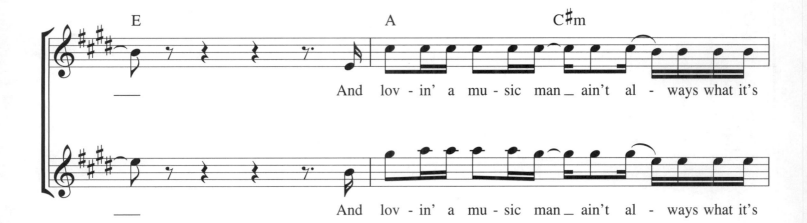

- 'ly. Right down the line, ___ it's been you ___ and me. ___

- 'ly. ___ Right down the line, ___ it's been you ___ and me. ___

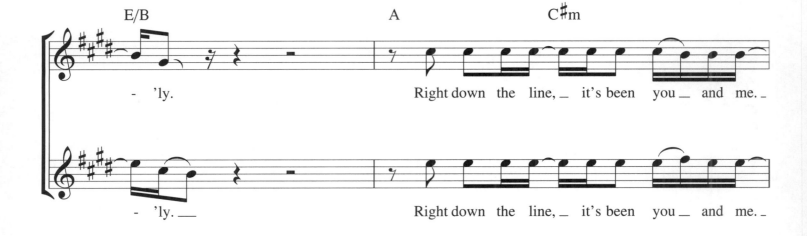

___ And lov - in' a mu - sic man ___ ain't al - ways what it's

___ And lov - in' a mu - sic man ___ ain't al - ways what it's

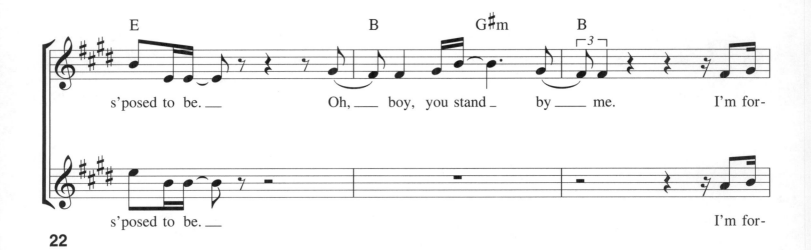

s'posed to be. ___ Oh, ___ boy, you stand ___ by ___ me. I'm for-

s'posed to be. ___ I'm for-

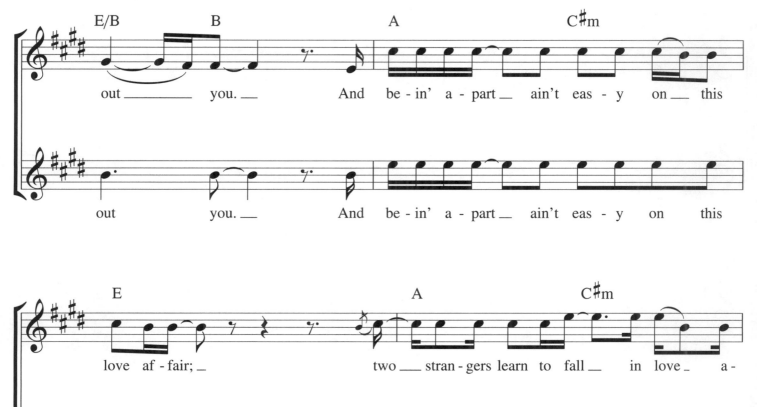

out _____ you. __ And be -in' a - part __ ain't eas - y on __ this

out _____ you. __ And be -in' a - part __ ain't eas - y on this

love af -fair; _ two __ stran - gers learn to fall __ in love __ a-

love af -fair; _ two __ stran - gers learn to fall __ in love __ a-

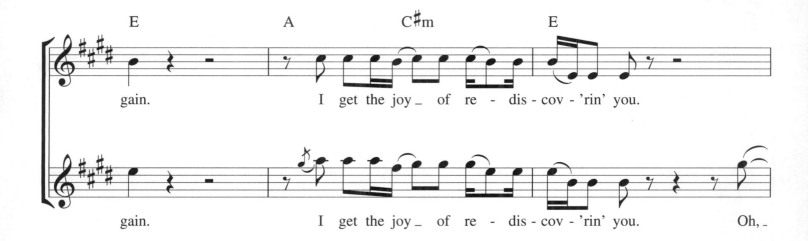

gain. I get the joy _ of re - dis - cov - 'rin' you.

gain. I get the joy _ of re - dis - cov - 'rin' you. Oh, _

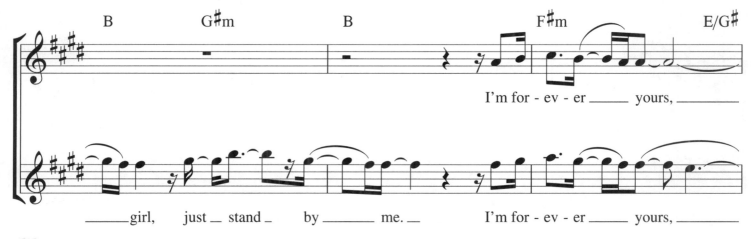

I'm for - ev - er _____ yours, _____

____ girl, just _ stand _ by ___ me. I'm for - ev - er ___ yours, ___

Interlude

faith-ful-ly. _____

faith-ful-ly. _____

Outro

Oh, _____ oh, _____

Oh, _____ oh, _____

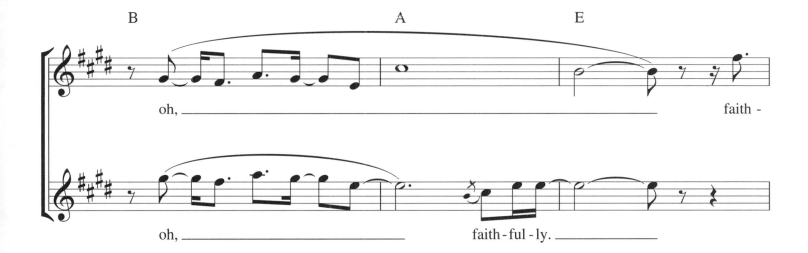

oh, _____ faith -

oh, _____ faith-ful-ly. _____

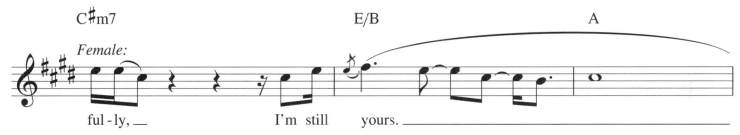

Female:

ful-ly, __ I'm still yours. _____

Gives You Hell

Words and Music by Tyson Ritter and Nick Wheeler

Copyright © 2008 by Universal Music - MGB Songs and Smells Like Phys Ed Music
All Rights Administered by Universal Music - MGB Songs
International Copyright Secured   All Rights Reserved

way, hope it gives you hell, hope it gives you _____ hell. ___ Now,

Verse

where's your pick - et fence, _ love, and where's that shin - y car, _

___ and did it ev - er get you _____ far? ___ You

nev - er seemed _ so tense, _ love; ___ I've nev-er seen you fall so

hard. Do you know where you are? ___ And

Pre-Chorus

truth be told, ___ I miss you. And

truth be told, ___ I'm ly - in'. When you see my

Chorus

face, hope it gives you hell, hope it gives you hell. When you walk my

28

way, hope it gives you hell, hope it gives you ___ hell. If you find a man ___

___ that's worth a damn ___ and treats you well, then he's a fool. ___

___ You're just as well, hope it gives you ___ hell, hope it gives you ___

Interlude

___ hell. To -

Verse

mor - row you'll ___ be think - in' to ___ your - self, ___ yeah, where did it all ___ go ___

Pre-Chorus

___ wrong? But the list goes on and on. ___ And truth be told, ___ I miss ___

___ you. And truth be told, ___ I'm ly - in'. When you see my

Chorus

face, hope it gives you hell, hope it gives you hell. When you walk my

way, hope it gives you hell, hope it gives you ___ hell. If you find a man ___

___ that's worth a damn ___ and treats you well, then he's a fool. ___

___ You're just as well, hope it gives you ___ hell. Now

Bridge

you'll _ nev-er see ___ what you've _ done _ to me. ___ You can

take back _ your mem-o-ries; they're no ___ good _ to me. ___ And

here's all ___ your lies, ___ you can look me in the eyes _ with that

sad, _ sad ___ look that you wear so well. ___

Chorus

Chorus

When you see my face, hope it gives you hell, hope it gives you ____ hell. When you walk my way, hope it gives you hell, hope it gives you ____ hell. When you hear this song ___ and sing a-long, _ well, you'll nev-er tell. _ Then you're a fool, ___ I'm just as well, hope it gives you _

Outro

____ hell. When you hear this song. I hope that it ____ will give you hell. You can sing a-long. ___ I hope that it will treat you well.

Hello
Words and Music by Lionel Richie

Copyright © 1983 by Brockman Music and Brenda Richie Publishing
All Rights Reserved   Used by Permission

see it in your smile. ___ You're all I've ___ ev-er want - ed, and my

arms are o - pen wide. ___ 'Cause you know just what to say, and you

know just what ___ to do, _____ and I want to ___ tell you so ___ much, ___

I love you. I

Verse

long to see ___ the sun - light in your ___ hair. ___

Some - times I feel ___ my heart ___ will o - ver-

flow. ___ Hel - lo, ___ I've just got to let you know. 'Cause I

Chorus

won - der where ___ you are, ___ and I won - der what you do. ___ Are you ___

some-where _ feel-in' lone - ly, or is some-one lov - in' you? ___ Tell me

how to win _ your heart, _ for I have-n't got a clue. _____ But

let me _ start by _ say-ing, _ I love ___ you. _ Is it me _

Chorus

___ you're look-ing for? _ 'Cause I won-der where _ you are, _ and I

won-der what ___ you do. ___ Are you ___ some - where _ feel-in' lone - ly,

some-one lov - in' you? _ Tell me how to win _ your heart, _ for I

have-n't got _ a clue, _____ but let me _ start by _ say-ing, _

Outro

I love you. _____

34

I Dreamed a Dream

from LES MISÉRABLES
Music by Claude-Michel Schönberg
Lyrics by Alain Boublil, Jean-Marc Natel and Herbert Kretzmer

Music and Lyrics Copyright © 1980 by Editions Musicales Alain Boublil
English Lyrics Copyright © 1986 by Alain Boublil Music Ltd. (ASCAP)
Mechanical and Publication Rights for the U.S.A. Administered by Alain Boublil Music Ltd. (ASCAP) c/o Joel Faden & Co., Inc.,
MLM 250 West 57th St., 26th Floor, New York, NY 10107, Tel. (212) 246-7203, Fax (212) 246-7217, mwlock@joelfaden.com
International Copyright Secured. All Rights Reserved. This music is copyright. Photocopying is illegal.
All Performance Rights Restricted.

I'll Stand by You

Words and Music by Chrissie Hynde, Tom Kelly and Billy Steinberg

© 1994 EMI MUSIC PUBLISHING LTD. trading as CLIVE BANKS MUSIC LTD., TOM KELLY SONGS and JERK AWAKE
All Rights for EMI MUSIC PUBLISHING LTD. trading as CLIVE BANKS MUSIC LTD. Controlled and Administered by
EMI APRIL MUSIC INC.
All Rights Reserved   International Copyright Secured   Used by Permission

-fess   could make me love you ___ less. ___   I'll stand by

Chorus

you,   I'll stand by ___ you. ___   Won't let no-bod-y hurt ___

___ you.   I'll stand _ by   you.

Verse

So,   if you're mad,   get mad. _____   Don't hold it all in-

- side; ___   come on and talk to   me _____   now.

Hey,   what you got   to hide? _____   I get an-gry, _

___ too.   Well, I'm a   lot   like you. ___   When you're _

Pre-Chorus

_____ stand - ing _____ at the cross - roads, don't know which path to choose, _ let me come

a - long. 'Cause e - ven if you're _ wrong, I'll stand _ by

Chorus

you, I'll stand by _____ you. Won't let no - bod - y hurt _

_____ you. _____ I'll stand by you. _____ Take me in, in - to your

dark - est ho - ur, and I'll nev - er de - sert _____ you. _ I'll stand _ by

Interlude

you. And

Pre-Chorus

when, when the night falls on you, ba - by, _ you're feel - in' all

a - lone, you won't be on your _ own. I'll stand _ by

Lean on Me

Words and Music by Bill Withers

Intro
Moderately

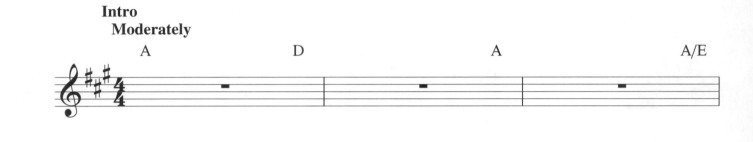

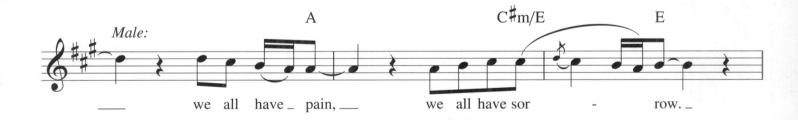

Yeah, _____ mm, _____

Oh. _____ oh, _____ oh, _____ no. Some - times in our lives, _

we all have _ pain, _ we all have sor - row. _

But if we are wise, _ we know that there's _ al - ways to - mor -

Copyright © 1972 INTERIOR MUSIC CORP.
Copyright Renewed
All Rights Controlled and Administered by SONGS OF UNIVERSAL, INC.
All Rights Reserved   Used by Permission

you need a hand. _ We all _ need some-bod-y to lean _____ on. _ I just

might have a prob-lem _ that you'll un-der-stand. _ We all _ need some-bod-y to lean _

Chorus

Female 1: _____ on. _ Lean on _ me when you're not strong, _

Male: Oh, _ lean on me, _____ hey,

_____ and I'll be your friend, _ I'll help you car-

when you're not strong, _____ I'll be your friend, ____

-ry _ on. _____ For it won't be long _

car - ry on and on and on and on. _____ Oh, _

Bridge 1

Verse

Bridge 2

46

Like a Prayer

Words and Music by Patrick Leonard and Madonna Ciccone

© 1988, 1989 EMI BLACKWOOD MUSIC INC., JOHNNY YUMA MUSIC, WB MUSIC CORP. and ORANGEJELLO MUSIC
All Rights for JOHNNY YUMA MUSIC Controlled and Administered by EMI BLACKWOOD MUSIC INC.
All Rights Reserved   International Copyright Secured   Used by Permission

Chorus 2

50

Chorus 2

Chorus 2

Interlude

Chorus 1

Hey.

Oh.

Hey.

Ooh.

Just like a dream, _ you are not what you _ seem. _

Just like a prayer, _ no choice, your voice can take me

Take me _

Outro
Freely

there.

there.

Like a Virgin

Words and Music by Billy Steinberg and Tom Kelly

Copyright © 1984 Sony/ATV Music Publishing LLC
All Rights Administered by Sony/ATV Music Publishing LLC, 8 Music Square West, Nashville, TN 37203
International Copyright Secured   All Rights Reserved

Verse

G6

Female 1:

all my love, __ boy, my fear is fad - ing fast. _____

Female 1:   Am

__ Been sav - ing it all ____ for __ you 'cause on - ly

Male:

Been sav - ing it all ____ for __ you 'cause on - ly

G6

love can last. ____ You're so fine, ___ and you're mine, __

love can last. ____ You're so fine, ___ and you're mine, __

____ make me strong, __ yeah, you make __ me bold. __ Oh, your

____ make me strong, __ yeah, you make __ me bold. __ Oh, your

Am   Em   Am

love thawed out, _____ yeah, your love thawed __ out _____

love thawed out, _____ yeah, your love thawed out _____

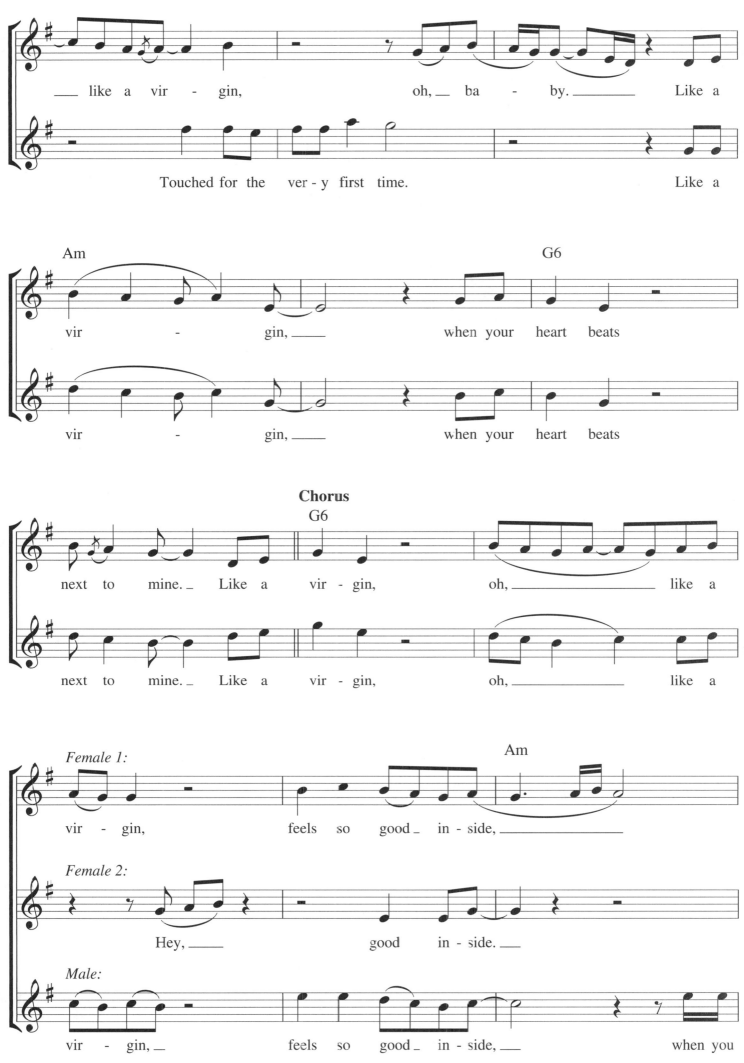

Chorus

61

Outro

My Life Would Suck Without You

Words and Music by Lukasz Gottwald, Max Martin and Claude Kelly

Copyright © 2009 Kasz Money Publishing, Maratone AB, Warner-Tamerlane Publishing Corp. and Studio Beast Music
All Rights for Kasz Money Publishing and Maratone AB Administered by Kobalt Music Services America, Inc.
All Rights for Studio Beast Music Administered by Warner-Tamerlane Publishing Corp.
International Copyright Secured   All Rights Reserved

said you'd nev - er come ___ back, ___ but

here you are ___ a - gain. ___ 'Cause we be - long ___

𝄋 Chorus

___ to - geth - er now, _____ yeah. ___ For - ev - er u - nit -

- ed here ___ some - how, _____ yeah. ___ You got a piece ___

___ of me ___ and hon - est - ly, ___ my ___ life

To Coda 𝄌 **Verse**

would suck with - out _____ you. ___ May - be I ___ was stu -

- pid   for   tell - in' you _ good - bye. __   May - be I __ was   wrong _

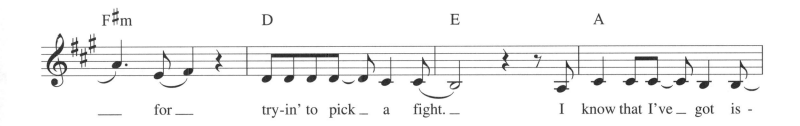

__ for __   try - in' to pick _ a   fight. __   I   know that I've _ got   is -

- sues,   but you're pret - ty messed _ up, too. __   Ei - ther way _ I   found _

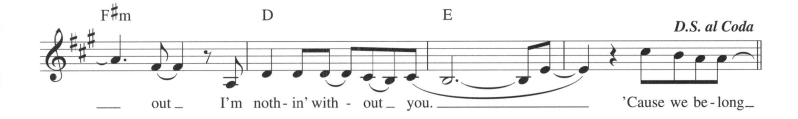

D.S. al Coda

__ out _   I'm noth - in' with - out _ you. _____ 'Cause we be - long _

Coda **Verse**

Be - in'   with __ you   is   so   dys - func - tion - al. __

__   I real - ly should - n't   miss __   you, _   but

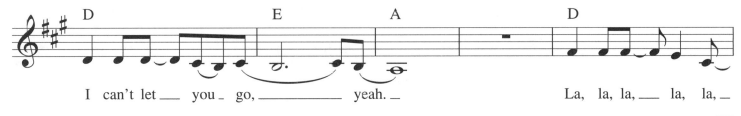

I   can't let __ you _ go, _____ yeah.   La, la, la, __ la, la, _

65

la, la, la, __ la, la, __ la. __ La, la, la, __ la, la. __

Chorus-Outro

'Cause we be-long __ to-geth - er now, __

__ yeah. __ For-ev-er u-nit - ed here __ some-how, __

__ yeah. __ You got a piece __ of me __

and hon-est-ly, __ my __ life would suck with-out __

__ you. __ 'Cause we be-long __ __

One

Lyrics by Bono and The Edge
Music by U2

Copyright © 1991 UNIVERSAL - POLYGRAM INTERNATIONAL MUSIC PUBLISHING B.V.
All Rights for the United States and Canada Controlled and Administered by
UNIVERSAL - POLYGRAM INTERNATIONAL PUBLISHING, INC.
All Rights Reserved   Used by Permission

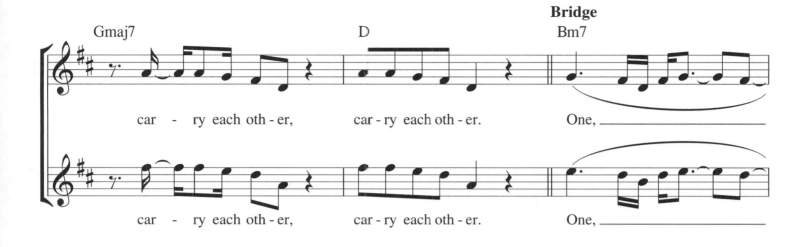

Chorus 1

71

Outro

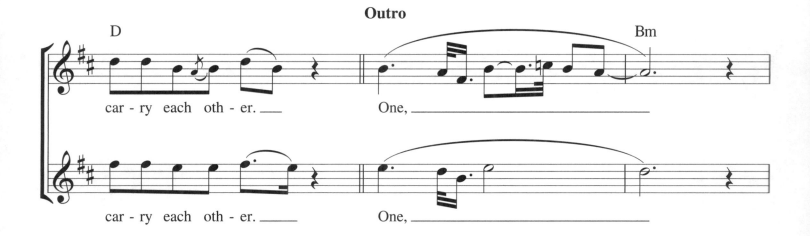

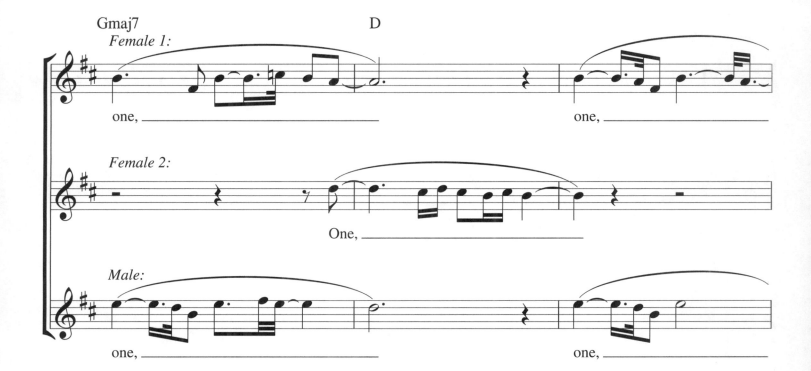

The Safety Dance

Words and Music by Ivan Doroschuk

* Spoken 1st time.

Copyright © 1983 SONGS OF UNIVERSAL, INC.,
UNIVERSAL - SONGS OF POLYGRAM INTERNATIONAL, INC. and BETTY SONGS
All Rights Controlled and Administered by SONGS OF UNIVERSAL, INC.
All Rights Reserved   Used by Permission

To Coda

We can dance, we can dance, we're do-in' it from wall to wall. _

We can dance, we can dance, ev-'ry-bod-y look at your hands. _

We can dance, we can dance, ev-'ry-bod-y's tak-in' the cha - ance. ___

___ Yeah, it's safe - ty dance, _ well, it's safe - ty dance, _

___. yeah, it's safe - ty dance. _

Verse

We can dance if we want to, _ we got all your life and mine, _ as long _

___ as we a - buse it, nev - er gon - na lose it, ev - 'ry-thing - 'll work out right. I say,

we can dance if we want to, __ we can leave your friends be-hind, __ 'cause your

D.S. al Coda

friends don't dance, and if ___ they don't dance, well, they're no friends of mine. __ I say,

Coda

__ Well, it's safe - ty dance, __ oh yeah, safe - ty dance, __

__ oh well, it's safe - ty dance, __ oh yeah, it's safe - ty dance, __

__ oh well, it's safe - ty dance, __ oh well, it's safe - ty dance. __

Outro

__ Oh, it's safe - ty dance, __ well, it's safe - ty dance, __

__ oh, it's safe - ty dance, __ I want safe - ty dance. __

Total Eclipse of the Heart

Words and Music by Jim Steinman

Copyright © 1982 by Lost Boys Music
All Rights for the United States and Canada Administered by Edward B. Marks Music Company
International Copyright Secured   All Rights Reserved
Used by Permission

Pre-Chorus

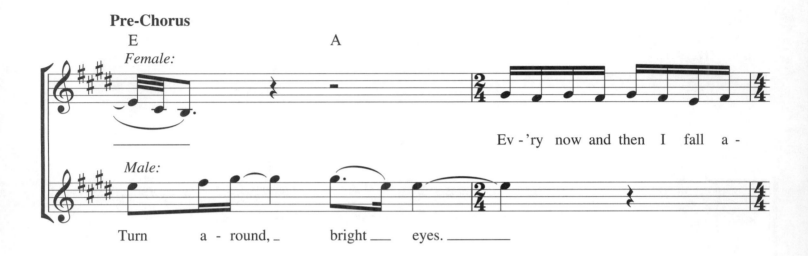

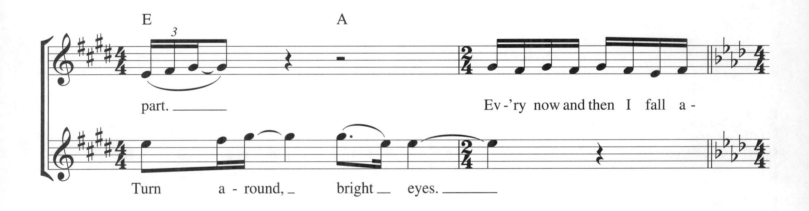

Chorus

ev - er. And we'll on - ly be mak - in' it right __ 'cause we'll nev-er be wrong. __ To-

geth - er we can take it to the end of the line; ___ your

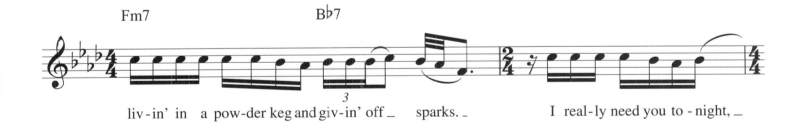

love is like a shad - ow on me all the time. _____ I don't __

___ know what to do, __ I'm al - ways in the dark. __ We're

liv-in' in a pow-der keg and giv-in' off __ sparks. _ I real-ly need you to - night, _

___ for - ev - er's gon - na start to - night. _

Once up-on a time, I was fall-ing in love, _ now I'm on-ly fall-ing a-part. _

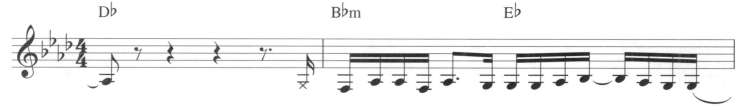

_ There's noth-in' I can do, a to-tal e-clipse _ of the heart. _

Female:
Once up-on a time, there was light in my life, _ now there's on-ly love in the dark. _

Male:
Now there's on-ly love in the dark. _

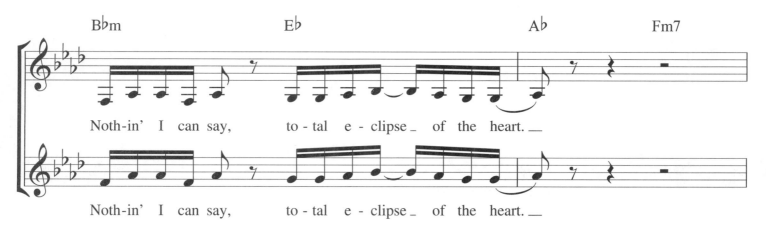

Noth-in' I can say, to-tal e-clipse _ of the heart. _

Noth-in' I can say, to-tal e-clipse _ of the heart. _

Interlude

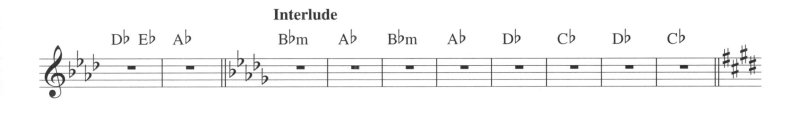

Pre-Chorus

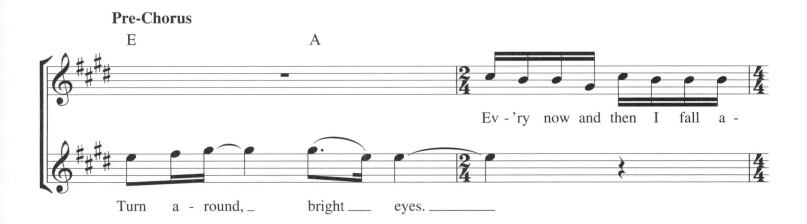

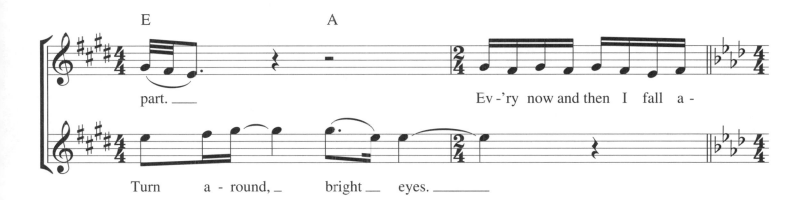

Chorus

geth - er we can take it to the end of the line; ___ your

love is like a shad-ow on me all of the time. _____ I don't ___

___ know what to do, ___ I'm al - ways in the dark. ___ We're

liv-in' in a pow-der keg and giv-in' off ___ sparks. _____ I real-ly need you to-night, _

for - ev - er's gon-na start _ to - night. ___

Once up-on a time, I was fall-ing in love, _ now I'm on-ly fall-ing a-part. _

Now I'm on-ly fall-ing a-part. _

There's noth-in' I can do, a to-tal e-clipse _ of the heart, _

There's noth-in' I can do, to-tal e-clipse _ of the heart, _

Outro

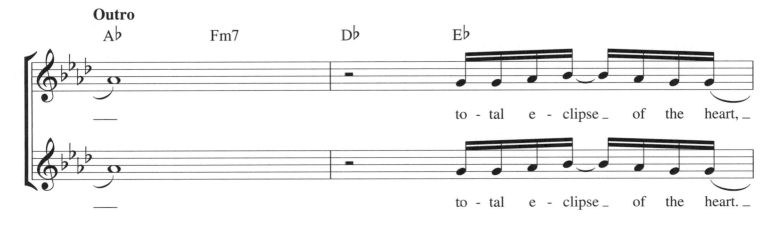

to-tal e-clipse _ of the heart, _

to-tal e-clipse _ of the heart. _

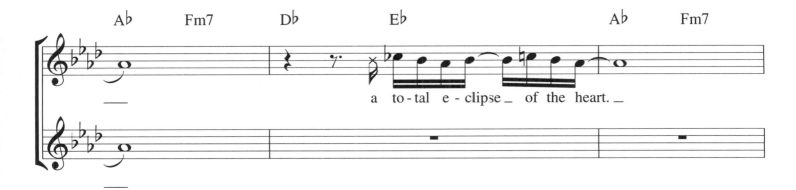

a to-tal e-clipse _ of the heart. _

Turn a-round, bright eyes.

True Colors

Words and Music by Billy Steinberg and Tom Kelly

Copyright © 1986 Sony/ATV Music Publishing LLC
All Rights Administered by Sony/ATV Music Publishing LLC, 8 Music Square West, Nashville, TN 37203
International Copyright Secured   All Rights Reserved

Pro Vocal® Series
SONGBOOK & SOUND-ALIKE CD
SING 8 GREAT SONGS WITH A PROFESSIONAL BAND

Whether you're a karaoke singer or an auditioning professional, the Pro Vocal® series is for you! Unlike most karaoke packs, each book in the Pro Vocal Series contains the lyrics, melody, and chord symbols for eight hit songs. The CD contains demos for listening, and separate backing tracks so you can sing along. The CD is playable on any CD player, but it is also enhanced so PC and Mac computer users can adjust the recording to any pitch without changing the tempo! Perfect for home rehearsal, parties, auditions, corporate events, and gigs without a backup band.

WOMEN'S EDITIONS

00740247	**1. Broadway Songs**	$14.95
00740249	**2. Jazz Standards**	$14.95
00740246	**3. Contemporary Hits**	$14.95
00740277	**4. '80s Gold**	$12.95
00740299	**5. Christmas Standards**	$15.95
00740281	**6. Disco Fever**	$12.95
00740279	**7. R&B Super Hits**	$12.95
00740309	**8. Wedding Gems**	$12.95
00740409	**9. Broadway Standards**	$14.95
00740348	**10. Andrew Lloyd Webber**	$14.95
00740344	**11. Disney's Best**	$14.99
00740378	**12. Ella Fitzgerald**	$14.95
00740350	**14. Musicals of Boublil & Schönberg**	$14.95
00740377	**15. Kelly Clarkson**	$14.95
00740342	**16. Disney Favorites**	$14.99
00740353	**17. Jazz Ballads**	$14.99
00740376	**18. Jazz Vocal Standards**	$14.95
00740375	**20. Hannah Montana**	$16.95
00740354	**21. Jazz Favorites**	$14.99
00740374	**22. Patsy Cline**	$14.95
00740369	**23. Grease**	$14.95
00740367	**25. ABBA**	$14.95
00740365	**26. Movie Songs**	$14.95
00740360	**28. High School Musical 1 & 2**	$14.95
00740363	**29. Torch Songs**	$14.95
00740379	**30. Hairspray**	$14.95
00740380	**31. Top Hits**	$14.95
00740384	**32. Hits of the '70s**	$14.95
00740388	**33. Billie Holiday**	$14.95
00740389	**34. The Sound of Music**	$15.99
00740390	**35. Contemporary Christian**	$14.95
00740392	**36. Wicked**	$15.99
00740393	**37. More Hannah Montana**	$14.95
00740394	**38. Miley Cyrus**	$14.95
00740396	**39. Christmas Hits**	$15.95
00740410	**40. Broadway Classics**	$14.95
00740415	**41. Broadway Favorites**	$14.99
00740416	**42. Great Standards You Can Sing**	$14.99
00740417	**43. Singable Standards**	$14.99
00740418	**44. Favorite Standards**	$14.99
00740419	**45. Sing Broadway**	$14.99
00740420	**46. More Standards**	$14.99
00740421	**47. Timeless Hits**	$14.99
00740422	**48. Easygoing R&B**	$14.99
00740424	**49. Taylor Swift**	$14.99
00740425	**50. From This Moment On**	$14.99
00740426	**51. Great Standards Collection**	$19.99
00740430	**52. Worship Favorites**	$14.99
00740434	**53. Lullabyes**	$14.99
00740438	**54. Lady Gaga**	$14.99

MEN'S EDITIONS

00740248	**1. Broadway Songs**	$14.95
00740250	**2. Jazz Standards**	$14.95
00740251	**3. Contemporary Hits**	$14.99
00740278	**4. '80s Gold**	$12.95
00740298	**5. Christmas Standards**	$15.95
00740280	**6. R&B Super Hits**	$12.95
00740282	**7. Disco Fever**	$12.95
00740310	**8. Wedding Gems**	$12.95
00740411	**9. Broadway Greats**	$14.99
00740333	**10. Elvis Presley – Volume 1**	$14.95
00740349	**11. Andrew Lloyd Webber**	$14.95
00740345	**12. Disney's Best**	$14.95
00740347	**13. Frank Sinatra Classics**	$14.95
00740334	**14. Lennon & McCartney**	$14.99
00740335	**16. Elvis Presley – Volume 2**	$14.99
00740343	**17. Disney Favorites**	$14.95
00740351	**18. Musicals of Boublil & Schönberg**	$14.95
00740346	**20. Frank Sinatra Standards**	$14.95
00740358	**22. Great Standards**	$14.99
00740341	**24. Duke Ellington**	$14.99
00740359	**26. Pop Standards**	$14.99
00740362	**27. Michael Bublé**	$14.95
00740361	**28. High School Musical 1 & 2**	$14.95
00740364	**29. Torch Songs**	$14.95
00740366	**30. Movie Songs**	$14.95
00740368	**31. Hip Hop Hits**	$14.95
00740370	**32. Grease**	$14.95
00740371	**33. Josh Groban**	$14.95
00740373	**34. Billy Joel**	$14.99
00740381	**35. Hits of the '50s**	$14.95
00740382	**36. Hits of the '60s**	$14.95
00740383	**37. Hits of the '70s**	$14.95
00740385	**38. Motown**	$14.95
00740386	**39. Hank Williams**	$14.95
00740387	**40. Neil Diamond**	$14.95
00740391	**41. Contemporary Christian**	$14.95
00740397	**42. Christmas Hits**	$15.95
00740399	**43. Ray**	$14.95
00740400	**44. The Rat Pack Hits**	$14.99
00740401	**45. Songs in the Style of Nat "King" Cole**	$14.99
00740402	**46. At the Lounge**	$14.95
00740403	**47. The Big Band Singer**	$14.95
00740404	**48. Jazz Cabaret Songs**	$14.99
00740405	**49. Cabaret Songs**	$14.99
00740406	**50. Big Band Standards**	$14.99
00740412	**51. Broadway's Best**	$14.99
00740427	**52. Great Standards Collection**	$19.99
00740431	**53. Worship Favorites**	$14.99
00740435	**54. Barry Manilow**	$14.99
00740436	**55. Lionel Richie**	$14.99

MIXED EDITIONS

These editions feature songs for both male and female voices.

00740311	**1. Wedding Duets**	$12.95
00740398	**2. Enchanted**	$14.95
00740407	**3. Rent**	$14.95
00740408	**4. Broadway Favorites**	$14.99
00740413	**5. South Pacific**	$15.99
00740414	**6. High School Musical 3**	$14.99
00740429	**7. Christmas Carols**	$14.99
00740437	**8. Glee**	$14.99

FOR MORE INFORMATION, SEE YOUR LOCAL MUSIC DEALER, OR WRITE TO:

7777 W. BLUEMOUND RD. P.O. BOX 13819 MILWAUKEE, WI 53213

Visit Hal Leonard online at www.halleonard.com

Prices, contents, & availability subject to change without notice.
Disney charaters and artwork © Disney Enterprises, Inc.

0910